A Bite-Sized Business Book

Profitable Partnerships

Practical Solutions to Help Pick the Right Business Partner

Stuart Haining ACIB, MCIM

Published by Bite-Sized Books Ltd 2019

Although the publisher and author have used reasonable care in preparing this book, the information it contains is distributed as is and without warranties of any kind. This book is not intended as legal, financial, social or technical advice and not all recommendations may be suitable for your situation. Professional advisers should be consulted as needed. Neither the publisher nor the author shall be liable for any costs, expenses or damages resulting from use of or reliance on the information contained in this book.

©Stuart Haining 2019

Bite-Sized Books Ltd Cleeve Croft, Cleeve Road, Goring RG8 9BJ
UK
information@bite-sizedbooks.com
Registered in the UK. Company Registration No: 9395379

The right of Stuart Haining to be identified as the author of this work has been asserted by him in accordance with the Copyright, Design and Patents Act 1988

ISBN: 9781797453651

Published by:

Bite-Sized Books Ltd
Cleeve Croft, Cleeve Road, Goring RG8 9BJ UK
information@bite-sizedbooks.com
Registered in the UK. Company Registration No: 9395379

Stuart Haining

Stuart Haining is an Award Winning Marketer, former Banker and Partnership Manager for Barclaycard, owner of several successful businesses, including a carbon-neutral ethical Internet Marketing Agency and a participant in many more. In fact a new opportunity or partner generally finds itself at his door roughly every 100 days or so!

Stuart has been involved in technical innovation for over two decades and cut his first partnership teeth almost 50 years ago when he was surprisingly ripped-off by a school friend! Fortunately this didn't put him off business altogether and he has since worked on several world-first projects, including the infamous shopping portal BarclaySquare, an early peer to Amazon.

He subsequently quit the Bank, partnered with a Venture Capital firm to launch new ideas online, was sacked by the company he founded, only to then participate in a MBO of one division of said company and eventually exit by selling out with his partner for several million to a PLC in 2010. Since then he has continued with an active policy of launching new businesses and finding more partners of his own.

It's fair then to say that Stuart has experienced a lot and that relationships with partners have been interesting, dramatic, stressful and ultimately fruitful.

Overall though he has enjoyed a lot more success with the good partnerships than he has lost through the bad ones and this Bite Sized book presents a unique opportunity to not just learn anecdotal advice about partnerships but also draw statistical conclusions from what must be an almost unparalleled number of 150+ real-life partner experiences garnered over a lifetime in this kind of business.

Stuart lives with his wife and daughter in Northamptonshire and in his spare time creates yet more *opportunities* or writes *cheeky little books** on topics from cars and marketing to innovation and business on the Internet.

*Quote from a proper author!

Paul Davies, Editor, Bite-Sized Books Limited

Contents

Stuart Haining

Introduction

My Credentials in Partnership

Ways to Start a Business

So What is a Partnership?

Why might you pick a Partnership?

So What Other Reasons Exist for Picking a Partnership Route?

Partnership Demographics

Partnership Frequency

Where to Find a Partner?

Partnership Pitfalls

Dodgy Deals

Partnership Upsides

Chances of Success?

Chances of Breakeven?

Chances of Failure / Overall Return?

Outcome in Chart Form

Best Partners to Pick

Worst Partners to Pick

Hints and Tips

With Hindsight

Legal View

    Template Business Agreement

    Template Acquisition Document

Bite-Sized Books

Bite-Sized Books Catalogue

Introduction

Starting a business venture seems to me to be a great way of putting structure into a hobby, which in turn can become great fun, a good way to meet new people and of course, if you are lucky, it's a great way to make money too. In fact my good friend Art Rain in his Bite-Sized Book *The Average Wage Millionaire* considers starting a business as probably the best way to make money with any degree of certainty.

This new Bite-Sized Book about Partnerships builds on that message by explaining how and why you might best use partnerships to your advantage, explores some reasons for making the effort in the first place and of course points out pitfalls observed first hand over the years. In some cases these are in the form of statistics – I have been involved in over 160 business relationships for various reasons (and this doesn't even include the numerous additional *normal* work colleagues), so it's a surprisingly large figure – so I probably have more than enough data on which to base some conclusions on the maths of partnerships alone. I will also include some examples of things that have gone well or otherwise for me and people I know in business.

I am of course never describing any specific person, relationship or partnership in detail as this simply wouldn't be fair to the other people involved in said relationships who don't have an equal voice to respond here, so I am instead aiming to describe instead more of a **caricature** or maybe an **avatar** is a better term to describe an amalgam of characteristics observed from across multiple relationships to make the necessary examples for you.

In addition I should add that this book is written mostly for a **UK** audience as the figures quoted are in pounds and the laws applying to business relate to the UK. That said, in a global economy I find that many similar elements exist in most advanced economies around the world so I have no reason to believe the lessons I have learnt first hand won't apply equally well in Europe or on the other side of the globe.

I hope you find my experiences and conclusions useful and good luck in which ever direction you decide to take your business.

My Credentials in Partnerships

As you can tell from my biography I first got involved in finding partners for business in my teens, but I was involved in what I would term proper partnerships when my then employer, Barclays, realised I had some good skills in this area.

Anyone who knows me will know I am neither the life and soul of the party nor the most sociable of people, but I am good at working out a **win-win** situation for the various parties to a deal – and then finding compromises between them without alienating each side, and this seems to work well when setting up and managing partnerships.

Maybe that's a win-win definition after all?

I have worked in the past with people whose view of business generally is the opposite of this and they think that success comes only from roughing other people up in negotiations: they aim for a **win-lose**. Negotiations frequently break down as a result whereas my approach is to try and give the other party something they value and I don't intentionally play games or try to be underhand – so a transparent approach really does reap rewards IMHO, even so, this won't stop me being a fierce negotiator, particularly when buying. In essence, though, I believe firmly that even if you don't reveal your full hand you can still avoid telling lies or half-truths in most cases.

I remember during negotiations to acquire the business which eventually made me a sizeable part of my small fortune I was asked a direct question about how much different people, including directors, were drawing from the business. In subsequent negotiations this was used against me to **leverage** up new people's wages so they ended up earning more than even the original staff in the acquiring business, so not good or a win-win?

But I learnt subsequently this data was checked for accuracy elsewhere and when proven to be correct, the assumption was made that all other details in the deal must be reasonably accurate too! Hence the acquisition deal got completed (when most thought it would fail at multiple difficult milestones) and as a result all parties ended up substantially better off overall years down the line.

During my varied career I have also been at the heart of negotiations to acquire almost a **dozen** businesses. In every case this has required careful communication and hand-holding with new business partners who need to be similarly convinced you are not intent on stealing their shirt or lunch. In many cases this has made deals extremely protracted and complicated and hence it has been very common for other directors, investors or staff to feel that the chances of a deal going all the way to fruition are **less than say 10%.** By carefully managing the process and way people feel they are being treated and respected, I would be surprised if my overall deal success rate was less than 90%, and at its heart this is all down to treating the individuals involved as if they are **trusted partners** and at the very least, equals, and certainly not adversaries.

The pinnacle of my partnership experience came when working for Barclaycard. I managed five marketing teams, each with a different function. One of these had a significant relationship with one of the UK's smallest but fastest growing motoring brands, conversely, Barclays Bank (our parent company) had an even bigger relationship with said company's main rival, the market leader. And this was a relationship so large it solely funded a whole region of the Bank's business and dated back a century. This business was alarmed at how fast the young upstart competitor was growing, partly aided by Barclaycard's patronage and reputation of course, so they issued an ultimatum to the Bank's Head Office, *resign this other business or we will take **all** our Group's business away* from Barclays Group.

The Bank's solution, which was very crafty but perhaps ingenious, was to hand me **both** relationships to manage **simultaneously**. This was real rock and a hard place stuff as I had to manage the Bank's very large client relationship alongside the fact I **also** managed the smaller competitor too which was a supplier to my teams – in short, I had to negotiate a path pleasing both brands who had declared war on each other, or else the Bank would no doubt have had few qualms sacking me as a sacrificial lamb!

Maybe that was their plan after all but it didn't work out that way!

I'm not sure how I did it but I ended up being taken (as one of only two guests) to the school re-union of the Bank client, that is a group director of the larger (angry) company, and as a result he ended up so happy we stayed working with him **and** we could keep working with his smaller competitor.

Said competitor is almost as big now so maybe not such a good decision on his part but I must be getting something right with my self-trained partner skills!

Ways to Start a Business

There are of course many and varied ways of starting out or setting up a business venture. In the UK it is common practice to start off, particularly if your business is based around a hobby or area of personal passion, to simply trade in cash or mixed through your normal household bills and income. And in fact the taxman is mindful of this and allows profits of **£1,000** each year from fledgling businesses, whatever the kind.

So it doesn't matter if you are selling on eBay, Amazon, Etsy or at craft-fairs, if you are only making pocket-money income, you can get started on your own as a **sole trader**, you don't need partners, you don't need hugely sophisticated accounts and processes and you probably don't really even need to tell anyone.

But as your business grows it does become important, in fact vital, to do things professionally by keeping accurate records, having separate bank accounts and producing regular accounts. It may even become necessary to borrow money for equipment, premises, stock or staff.

> **NB.** One reason for this is I believe if the tax man catches you with a business bigger than this and not declaring your full figures, they can **guestimate** what the business might be trading, and tax on that made up estimate –

and no surprises, they won't pick a small number. Why would they. So avoidance can end in **costing more.**

At this point a business starts to create **risk**. There is a risk for other companies to transact with you, and this in turn creates a risk that can spill down to you personally. So it's important to ensure you are protecting yourself as if the business hits a bump in the road and, say, runs out of cash or has a big client who fails to pay, the debts that mount up as a result will be owed by you **personally**, even if they relate solely to your business. So you could end up bankrupt and lose your home, car, cash and everything as all your assets legally can be **lumped together**.

This leads many people to set up in business as a **Limited Company,** and I too have done this many times. In this scenario the company issues a few shares and allocates these to key people involved with the business, for example the founders who will also be directors. There are many ways of allocating different levels of rights and responsibilities to these directors but common features are that the assets of the business are split between the shareholders in **proportion** to the number of shares held.

As an example, in my current main company, the online marketing agency, every year we double the shareholding and give away free shares to whoever has contributed most to our success – in general this will be to my family and key colleagues but outside partners also benefit, as do former employees, and the more they keep contributing the more they can grow their share of the company and its corresponding share of either assets or dividends. Each type of shareholder has a different class of share to which attach different rights, and in most cases they receive dividends at a rate proportional to my own.

In addition a very important factor is that the company takes on responsibility for its own trading and risk, so, irrespective of the number of shares owned (and let's assume paid for) all risks will attach **solely** to the company unless of course you act fraudulently. If it goes bust, the company assets only get sold to pay off debts and your personal assets are ring-fenced and safe – so in short your risk is **Limited**, hence the term Limited Company.

This applies unless of course you have separately pledged your personal name and assets as security also for the company!

> **NB.** Do not rush into doing this as it's a lot harder to exit such an arrangement than it is to start one, I know to my cost and nearly lost the house!
>
> **Editor's note:** I gather there are alternatives anyway?
>
> **Author's note:** Absolutely. Whilst bankers don't like it and often refuse, you can try instead to get them to loan money using a **lien** (ownership entitlement) over the **company's own assets, such as stock or book-debts**, in preference to chasing you for money. In a

former company I achieved this by **voluntarily** pre-valuing our assets at only **20%** of the real value which was enough of a drop in margin to enable the bankers to realise they could sell our assets, even in a hurry, and still more than cover the debt, so they had very little room to refuse a deal. And they couldn't use different figures as 20% was pragmatic enough anyway (and I had a good idea it was similar to their own mark-down rates used internally to control Bank risk).

And having a company to protect you isn't even that expensive – most decent accountants can be employed for around **£100** a month.

Another way of setting up in business, and in many ways it's similar to a company, is to set up as a **LLP**. This stands for Limited Liability Partnership and as the name implies it offers some of the same protection in the same way as a Limited Company but personal assets can still be captured, so it can have some risk.

Such schemes are generally used by **professional** services firms such as lawyers and accountancy firms (and I too have been involved in one of these) where individuals are buying their way into an established business and can't simply draw or commit assets back out of the arrangement. But LLP's don't have all the same rights, responsibilities and rules as companies so shouldn't be entered into lightly.

> **Editor's note:** Why pick an LLP over a Limited?

> **Author's note:** I'm not completely sure but I do believe some of the tax treatment rules are beneficial if you are employed via an LLP instead of a company, and it works better for company cars too! Plus the administration and audit costs each year can be a bit lower than a company arrangement. I prefer limited companies.

This then leads nicely on to the other main way of trading in business, (beyond being a sole trader on your own of course which I have mentioned is the most popular option in the UK) and that is in a traditional **Partnership**. This could be an informal relationship between family or friends, or as I prefer, a loosely organised (but still carefully structured) **legal agreement** between individuals and companies. And at the top end you can have a legal agreement as comprehensive as an LLP or Limited Company.

I tend to structure my deals as a Marketing Joint Venture but they are really a partnership by another name, albeit I do aim to restrict their reach into my personal assets within the business agreement.

So What Is a Partnership?

Many definitions of partnership are given by business groups, HM revenue and Customs (for tax purposes), the Banks (for Agreement purposes) and to a degree I disagree with most of these as they assume everyone has a rigid arrangement and generally **shared** contribution and risks. I think the beauty of a partnership is in fact that it can be made to be flexible enough to accommodate almost *any* different combination of factors that suit your own goals, both personal and business, but I will say more on this throughout the book and at the end I have shared an example of quite a complex arrangement where I was aiming to achieve just a minority stake in a new venture as my skills weren't the biggest part of the venture.

So for me, Wikipedia has probably the most balanced description of what a partnership is all about, as follows:

> *A partnership is an arrangement where parties, known as partners, agree to cooperate to advance their **mutual interests**. The partners in a partnership may be individuals, businesses, interest-based organisations, schools, governments or combinations. Organisations may partner to increase the likelihood of each achieving their **mission** and to **amplify** their reach. A partnership may result in issuing and holding **equity** or may be only governed by a **contract**.*

Perfect.

To me it confirms you have **mutual interests, a goal or mission to achieve, and you want to leverage or amplify your results.** But that's it. It doesn't limit members of the partnership to any arrangements where everybody invests the same in skills or cash, or even limit it to an arrangement involving shares, it states equity (ownership percentages) could be a factor but equally it could be just a contract – so a letter or memorandum of understanding. In short, anything you could put in front of a lawyer or court will probably suffice.

In my case I have formed many fledgling business ventures by creating a simple **Agreement in Principle** or **Heads of Terms** based around a core legal document written at low cost by a **Notary Public** – so legal costs were in the hundreds of pounds, not thousands, and many of the deals or prospective deals were based around a **single** generic template with just the participants, numbers and business purpose varying in each case so that every arrangement can be as flexible as your imagination. I will share an example of this later in the book but you should of course seek your own legal representation.

> **NB.** This is one way I have minimised my costs and losses in business as out of circa 160 partnership opportunities I have been involved with, circa **30% have died prior to Agreement stage** and the supposed desire to work together was killed off in the negotiation

stage (so better to have wasted just a few pounds on a template Agreement adaptation than spending thousands on a bespoke Agreement each time with lawyers). And isn't it better to fall out with prospective partners at this early stage over small print and commercial terms than later on when you are invested in both effort and money?

Editor's note: Have you drawn any conclusion from this high reject rate?

Author's note: I have, and this is assuming it's not just a negative view on my personality or that I am difficult to work with! (I've asked a few people and they say I'm OK to work with!). So my conclusion here is that a lot of people think and talk big but never expect to get around to doing anything, especially anything formal, so when quickly presented with something that looks legal, they get forced off the fence and drop out rather than have to actually do something real for a change!

A further **10% of opportunities died before full implementation** could be accomplished – so those lower legal costs per deal is again a useful approach as it **saved me money in at least 40%** of cases, more if I include the ventures that only ever got as far as Break-Even.

Why Might You Pick a Partnership?

I have already discussed some of the technical reasons as to why a Partnership gets selected as an alternative to running a business as a Sole Trader, LLP or Limited Company and of course many other options exist including setting up as a **Charity / Not For Profit, Social Enterprise or Co-operative** for example. In the main these have financial and legislative implications and in some cases there is simply no option but to select a specific format.

However, picking a Partnership is a very specific lifestyle choice and I'd like to explore here some of the emotive reasons for making the choice to bring extra people into the ownership of your business and let's forget reasons such as legislation or tax advantages and risk.

To get us started I will share my own rationale as it's probably fair to say I have formed more partnership type deals than any other out of the options available (I've tried most others but gave up starting a charity – boy is it hard to get fair-priced advice then!)

I would like to think I am a very hard-working and driven individual, less so perhaps as I get older, but I think nothing of working evenings, weekends as required. I also rarely give in if a task is ahead of me and I can be something of a perfectionist, although again this is declining with age! However, in addition to these personality or business traits I know that I also have a natural and preferred tendency (given the chance) to be lazy plus I have a big fear of letting other people down.

So my reason for preferring to have business partners versus say setting up as a sole trader is simple. I fear that if I go it alone my lazy side may take precedence and I will not have the commitment to battle on (despite normally being very committed and hardworking) and hence I pick a partner route as I know my **fear of letting them down** in our joint business will **outweigh my desire to be lazy**. In short, having a partner **forces me to be self-motivated** and get things done from which all partners benefit.

Weird I know – I'm part doing it for them but really also doing it for myself!

So What Other Reasons Exist for Picking a Partnership Route?

Family – this is arguably the most common route as people prefer to employ spouses, partners or children as the business grows and this is probably due to the perceived flexibility, re working hours and transport.

Friends – It is common to work with friends, often gained through work or a shared hobby or interest area, and this is for exactly that reason: you have a shared interest or skills.

Investment – It is common to seek a partner who can put capital in the business. This does not mean they also need to be an active participant, they could have minimal day-to-day involvement and be a sleeping partner contributing advice when asked and happy to take a reward when the business eventually sells or exits, or in the interim via dividends.

> **NB.** An old colleague of mine advised me his mother invested £10,000 like this when Asda first started out as a co-operative between farmers and as it grew she regularly received dividend cheques for hundreds of thousands of pounds. but had zero day to day dealing whatsoever with the business. But it wouldn't have got off the ground without her and eventually of course they sold out to Wall Mart – she must have made a fully justified (IMHO) packet then for taking the risk.

Skills – It is very common to form a Partnership with someone who has the missing piece of the jigsaw technically so that together you can compete with bigger companies

Sales – By this I really mean access to networking or lists of contacts rather than just sales skills, but again having a partner who has the contacts to make the business grow is an essential part of success for many businesses.

Earn Out – Sometimes the only way to get your hands on a business you want to acquire is by negotiating a deal to gradually enable the existing owners to exit, so they may take some cash out on day one and then take further tranches as their own involvement in the day to day running of the business dwindles.

Earn In – It is sometimes necessary to award a small shareholding to key new members of staff when they join, generally this is to entice them to come from larger competitors, and they can lock good employees in.

A word of warning here – this is hard to unpick unless like my company you keep on doubling shares or equity (so you can eventually dilute down the importance of anyone not contributing) so it's probably best to only do this when you have seen proven results after a decent period of time.

Suppliers – Having a key supplier or manufacturer or any firm that is critical to your success on board can be a good way of securing priority treatment or better prices, provided of course they don't give away your intellectual property or other secrets or hold you back on purpose. Again, best then to only do this after results are proven.

Partner Demographics

Whilst it will certainly be true that to some extent the relationships I have formed over the years with a view to forming a partnership (or actually forming one) will be driven by my own personality and traits, given that a proportion of the potential partners have sought me out proactively. there must be also a potential that the demographic I have seen is not in fact skewed or biased in any way but it is in fact more representative of the market potential as a whole and my relationships are therefore a good benchmark?

So what was the profile **overall**?

Gender.

Sadly 85% of the 160 or so relationships were males, only 13% were females, these being based on status at birth. 2% were from businesses.

Whether this is representative of the glass ceiling generally or the fact that males are more likely to be risk takers, I don't know. What I do know is that generally I get on better with women at work (as I am not a blokey bloke) so don't consider this to be a bias I have set out to create, in fact the opposite is probably true.

Age.

With one or two exceptions I found it interesting to note that in the vast majority (80%+) of cases the age of the prospective partner is always within **10 years**

either way of my own at the time. So this translates into the following pattern:

3% were under 20 years of age. (Obviously this result will be skewed by my own young age at the start!).

7% were under 30 years of age.

20% were under 40 years of age.

30% were aged between 40 and 50 years of age.

48% were aged between 50 and 65 years of age.

Only 2% were over 65 years old.

And a surprising **10% were approximately 55 years old** – this must be the golden age for doing deals and maybe it represents another hitherto undiscovered mid-life crisis! This assumes of course that you can get the deal live before aged 65 when inertia seems to set in big time! Obviously not all pensioners or 55 year olds are the same!

Occupation.

Only **5%** of the potential business partners came from what I would term blue-collar job roles as distinct from **managerial or professional**. A large proportion were of course business owners and directors. Circa 6% of these were from outside the UK although some of these people had recently moved into the UK to commence work.

Partnership Frequency

It is probably unsurprising to discover that some people are plainly serial partnership material / business starters (me included) and others less so, as on average each person got involved in **1.3 opportunities through me**. Most of course get involved in just one, but some people up to half a dozen business concepts, plus I'm sure they would be involved with more besides any involvement via me.

The actual number of opportunities embarked upon or considered **closely mirrored** the number of potential partners (as people) as whilst most businesses required more than one partner, some partners (as detailed above) get involved with more than one thing!

Beyond this I found it interesting to see that my own tendency to get involved with opportunities did increase and grow **over the years** and presumably this is as a result of my contact network widening all the time, my skills and knowledge (and general usefulness) also increasing, and maybe, too, an element of increased awareness? I think once you are of a mindset to get involved with new things you become better attuned to **hearing** of new opportunities and seeking them out, and to a degree they **find you** as a result of reaching into the universe.

Makes me sound like a Scientologist!

As you can see from the graph mapping my own encounters across almost 50 years, the opportunities to work with partners has steadily increased each year, also reaching a peak slightly before my own mid-fifties.

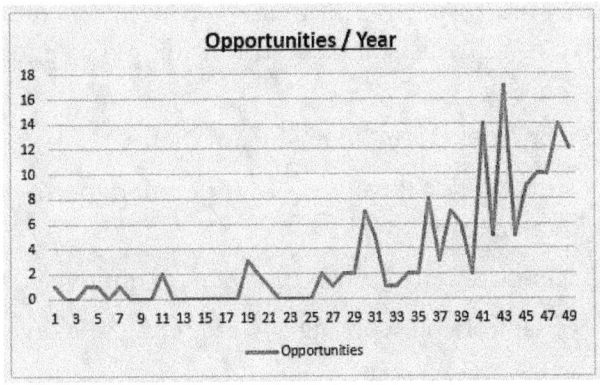

Editor's note: So let me get this correct, you are saying in your mid-fifties you were being approached to take part in business opportunities over **once a month**?

Author's note: Yes, although in many cases I was also the main instigator of the first discussions.

Where to Find a Partner

Across this lengthy period of study it would appear that the general breakdown as to the source of each partner or prospective partner was roughly as follows (I say roughly as some could fit multiple categories over time):

20% were introduced to me by associates

10% were work colleagues, e.g. different departments of the same company.

10% were from my own pool of staff / employees

10% came from networking and attending sales events

10% were from supplier companies

5% were clients or former clients

Broken down with greater granularity the precise source of partners over said 50 year span was as follows(and I'll provide further clarity of any salient points regarding each after this table):

SOURCE	RATIO
Introduced	17%
Supplier	12%
Networking	11%
Staff	10%
Colleagues	8%
My Search	6%
Clients	5%
Bosses	4%
Takeovers	4%
They Searched for Me	3%
Training	3%
Blagging	2%
Entrepreneurs	2%
Family	2%
MLM	2%
Neighbours	2%
Academics	1%
Companies	1%
Friends	1%
Investors	1%
Just Me	1%
Partners	1%
School	1%
	100%

Let's look then at each in more detail.

Introduced – as it says on the tin, these people were recommended to talk to me about partnering on a new business venture or just generally introduced in the normal course of business.

Supplier – These are people supplying products or services to whichever company I worked for at the time. In some cases I will have approached them, in just as many, they have approached me (suggesting we work together) first.

Networking – Contacts made at general networking or sales events such as conferences and via Membership Clubs such as BNI or the Chamber of Commerce.

Staff – People that work either directly for me as reports, or as members of teams that report indirectly into me, either in companies I worked for, such as HSBC, Barclays, DotDigital, or in my own businesses (which at one point employed 55 FTE).

Colleagues – Peers within businesses, most often only **passing** acquaintances meeting, say, in-passing monthly rather than close contacts talking daily.

My Search – I have a project in mind, have identified a skills or resource gap and have **actively** set about researching to find a suitable partner, either through existing contacts or by searching online via Google, LinkedIn or Companies House.

Clients – Senior staff or directors of companies that have been client customers of either my various companies or the businesses I have worked for. This will also include the occasional former client when they have chosen to seek me out years after working together in a prior business.

Bosses – As the title suggests these are my former bosses, ranging from line managers through to directors, not current bosses though as I don't have one!

> **Editor's note:** What about Mrs H at home.
>
> **Author's note:** Gosh, yes. Mustn't forget that important boss.

Takeovers – Over the years I have been involved in around a dozen business acquisitions and one of the strategies behind this was that with each new business acquisition we could **attract good new people** into the business (and jettison any that weren't so good of course before they joined!). This was the source of half a dozen potential partners.

They Searched for Me – As it says, people that searched for my expertise in places like LinkedIn or Google, most probably the former, or via network contacts and *word of mouth*.

Training – A similar number of people were connected at various training **courses, seminars and sales events** or trade exhibitions.

Blagging – Sad to say I have been known to try and open a few doors into new prospect companies and / or individuals that I don't know (but perceive a knowledge gap / need to get to know) by **pretending**

we have worked together or met years before. This had led to more than a few interesting long term opportunities all predicated on the basis that most of us are simply too busy to recall everything we have ever done. The key of course is good research in advance to ensure you are appropriately briefed about what the target actually does or did in the past. Hobbies and interests help with this kind of dialogue too.

> **Editor's note:** You should be ashamed!
>
> **Author's note:** It's not that bad. I know of at least one company where they have created forged uniforms to access competitor company premises so by contrast, my business should be in the Vatican! And we have never lied about anything, they assumed we'd met / worked together by the way things were said, such as, *Lovely to see you <u>again.</u> Seems ages since Earls Court Trade Show.* (Which is true.) I can't really be blamed if they read into that we'd met there before!

Entrepreneurs – Business Owners and Inventors of ideas are a pretty obvious source of potential partner as most fully realise they don't possess all the skills they need themselves.

Family – I had a few attempts at engaging both close and distant parts of the family (immediate as well as by marriage) into different opportunities and **none of these** ever went anywhere. It was perhaps no bad thing as I know from contacts in family businesses and investors / advisors on the outside that these are very tricky businesses to be involved with due to all manner of family squabbles, power battles, agendas, egos and ultimately different views on risk, success and exit.

> **Editor's note:** I've also heard it said that contrary to what you'd expect, that family are most likely to want to see relatives succeed, they are often the least likely and intentionally take action to hold other family members back!
>
> **Author's note:** I've heard that too. It's sometimes to do with rivalry but also often to do with being comfortable with you in a specific box, that is uncomfortable with change. Who would have expected that your biggest supporters could in fact be your biggest detractors. It's certainly food for thought when it comes to looking for partners – I'd suggest go elsewhere first!

MLM – Otherwise known as **Multi-Level-Marketing** or **Network Marketing** or Networking (but not the same at all as business networking at breakfast meetings of tradespeople). This is where by referral you are introduced to products and services that are sold by a direct sales model often (slightly incorrectly) described as a pyramid, hence it's also called **Pyramid Marketing**.

Introducers earn commission on their own sales and a smaller proportion on the sales of those they introduce to the business, known as the downline. I have trialled and researched many networks over the years ranging from Amway and FLP to Utility Warehouse and VWD, plus at one point I was a co-Director of a new shopping based MLM business (similar to Amazon but sadly not as successful!) and through all of these I have made many interesting friendships and found more than a few partnership and business prospects.

Neighbours – Pretty obvious that these could be a good source of partners as you may have **similar** goals, aspirations and lifestyles (as you presumably live in similar houses) but as the years progress you can't count on this. The old Acorn marketing profiling system groups people by factors like that and the groups are actually increasingly becoming very **disparate** as families separate and reform, single people live in big houses, large families crowd into small flats. So check out things carefully before assuming everybody near you is the same.

Academics – Through attending various courses and gaining qualifications since finishing my own further education I have met several academics, and a surprising number have an interest in extracurricular business activities these days, probably as a result of pressure on funding, meaning they have to be more business focussed simply to survive, as state funds won't pay for everything they need to do. In my experience these have always been great people to work with and learn from, and commercially in most cases they are extremely **fair** and **transparent**, which makes a nice change in business.

Companies – A small number of companies have entered into what I would call partnership arrangements with me – in the main this is still a deal with an individual, they just happen to represent **themselves** as a Limited Company. I started out like this when doing ongoing consultancy for the PLC that acquired our marketing agency – the deal was with me but I invoiced through a new company set up especially for that purpose, simply to limit my risk and ring-fence things for the taxman. Said company then morphed into my current agency but trades under a different name. I have never found large companies very open to the idea of partnering on new ideas – they all seem to hide behind having R&D Departments at the same time as the management themselves decry the lack of innovation with their own businesses!

Friends – It's inevitable that friends will be a possible source of partners in business, especially if you have the kind of relationship with them where discussions can be fairly free-ranging and hence will encompass business as well as areas of shared interest. I was surprised when compiling all this data at the low percentage of partners and prospective partners that came from this source though. It was a **lot less** than I anticipated before doing the maths.

Investors – These range from one-man band hobby investors such as myself through to professionally run, but small, private equity investors.

Just Me – I'm not sure how I ended up in the maths unless this relates to a partnership project which I eventually decided I would be better off flying solo, but it only impacted one project so let's not sweat the small stuff!

Partners – As the name suggests partners themselves can introduce further partners, from which it is then possible to branch out into yet more opportunities which sometimes may also again involve the original introducer, but not always. It is of course good form to keep them updated and / or invite them anyway.

<u>**School**</u> – This must date back to my earliest partnership experiments when I was at school. Despite on occasion reconnecting with old school contacts lost over the decades I have never tried nor expected this to be an obvious source of potential partners, even if research suggests the skills gap can be filled by such a person, for the simple reason that the time gap is too long and any approach to discuss business out of the blue would seem decidedly **dodgy**, even if it wasn't (I did try once and it didn't feel good). I think this is an area that therefore needs further exploring before a definitive answer can be given – but by becoming more involved with friends again first.

Surely if you found you could trust somebody twenty years ago, they are most probably a similar person today, ethically speaking anyway, but who knows what may have shaped them since?

You may disagree.

Partnership Pitfalls

I will now combine some of my own learning plus that from other contacts to create the aforementioned avatar personalities and explain some of the pitfalls observed with partnerships over the years. In this way I am not describing any one person and hence hopefully won't upset anyone who thinks I am talking about them.

I'm not!

And then in a section later about Fraud I will talk about some real life disasters which hopefully will reveal some useful learning should you decide to get into partnerships yourself.

The Mouth

The relationship starts off amazingly well, almost too well in fact, only to subsequently discover that those that shout loudest about what they are going to achieve **won't actually follow through**. This can be seen in the very high proportion of deals that's falter the minute any bit of paperwork (in the form of some kind of structured agreement, however fairly written and balanced it is) is put in front of them to review and sign. Plus the deals that fall apart due to inaction not long afterwards, so that's around **40%** of partnership potential that I have seen first-hand.

In my experience these failures were almost never caused by lack of initial effort on my part. I was the

impacted party, not the main cause. It's certainly yet another of those 80/20 scenarios and in my case I honestly always try to follow through with what I say I will do.

The Head-In-the-Sand.

Similar things have occurred with people conveniently *ignoring* (after the business has progressed, which you've helped with) that you did in fact have a **commission** or revenue sharing deal in place or were supposed to be allocated **equity** at a later date! Life is too short to dwell on this kind of thing and so far I have never resorted to legal means or the courts to re-enforce deals like this even though I am pretty sure the paperwork would support ruling in my favour. I prefer instead to move onto something more positive and succeed without hassle somewhere else.

Friends and colleagues have confirmed this has happened to them too but it's probably noteworthy to add that this kind of thing has happened to me *only 4 times* out of over seventy deals that did progress and make progress, so that's about **6% reject rate** suggesting you can't always rely on people as when they succeed they may just conveniently leave you behind.

> **NB.** I'm sure some people could lay a claim such as this at my door too but in my defence I would add that anything that may have felt like a rejection (unless they were swinging the

lead) or dodgy deal on my part was unintentional or simply a miscommunication. I have in fact often tried to reward past partners with equity in new ventures. In my current company we still pay dividends to former colleagues who had left many years earlier (or offer to buy them out at a fair market price) or I have tried to track down past partners, sadly often to no avail. So hand on heart I can say I haven't **ever** tried to diddle anyone intentionally.

The Memory Loss

I have experienced a situation where a deal is all agreed, paperwork approved, project plan and responsibilities approved and work then progresses with outside **contractors** (which has to be paid for) and rather foolishly I've fronted the money myself on the assumption that participants will willingly cough up their agreed share upon demand later. Only to discover that about **33%** then conveniently fail to remember they owe any money, **even when chased** and reminded of the agreement **multiple times**. So they never pay and may never have intended to, it's very disheartening amongst people you considered not just as partners but friends.

This wouldn't be so bad if partnering with people who have hit hard times, before or after, and they simply can't afford to pay or else they will starve.

This isn't what happened to me, I am talking about is well off people who **can** easily afford to pay a few hundred pounds each, but don't or won't rather than can't. Ditto very wealthy people who also never seem to have their cheque book or online banking details with them – and obviously don't respond to email reminders. They simply **prevaricate** and get away with it at somebody else's expense.

On more than one occasion such surprising behaviour has left me in the line of fire with the supplier as I was the one commissioning the work and the **only contact point**, and to do the decent thing I have had to pay up despite knowing I probably won't collect the money in from supposed partners to recoup my own losses. It should be said that to counteract this some very **kind partners**, upon hearing of such an occurrence, are super and volunteered to reduce the debt caused by others by paying a larger contribution than needed themselves, so they share the burden, but I was still significantly out of pocket.

The lesson here is two-fold, **don't lead from the front with suppliers** on your own – either ensure work is booked in multiple names, or get the money first, and if this isn't practical start work off in **small chunks** rather than go all out on a project until you see the colour of partners' money for real. We have carried this strategy, sadly forced by circumstance, across into our marketing agency today and now won't ever start work until an initial 20% is paid up-front – and it does seem to sort the wheat from the chaff and as I write this a supposed new client has suddenly been found wanting, and that's for just £100 set-up, but at least it saves us wasting time and effort. It's just a shame it's necessary.

The Lazy Ones

These are often those partners who again talk a good game and can exhibit all the right body language or use the right words in meetings to look keen and enthused only to then **deliver zero** once work begins. In fact it's worse than that as they actually waste your own precious time.

Often they've partnered up for other reasons and these can be as varied as helping them look or feel good or maybe they feel they will gain some other advantage by being involved in something new, perhaps as a Plan B, but all along Plan A was their game.

I have had to sack **3 or 4** partners out of businesses for lack of performance and it's never nice, even though they must realise they've contributed nothing but turn up to a few meetings. Needless to say the broader long-term relationship probably won't survive either outside of the failed partnership as few people will react well after being told they are a waste of space and effort!

The Brown-Nose

These can be partners who are suppliers who must feel that one way of ingratiating themselves and hanging onto contracts is by trying to align themselves with their customer's private and personal goals - even though they have no real interest themselves either personally or in a business capacity. So again, these are partners solely to look good and win some **brownie points.**

The Career Ladder

This is a close relative of the Brown-Nose and is a warning to avoid members of staff fawning interest for similar reasons. They think it will please you and help them on their own career ladder towards promotion for the Plan A job which they have with you – so this kind of false partner is most likely if you start a business whilst working in a bigger business and the partnership project is itself a Plan B for you but they are all about Plan A.

The Boss

And here I don't mean your spouse as this is an interesting take in reverse on the Career Ladder partner and I have heard of situations where employees get **embroiled** in new start-up and partner discussions with their bosses. It's obviously **flattering** to be courted by your boss in the first place, and also difficult to refuse as surely won't that have the reverse effect on your chances of rising up the career ladder? So you'd better do it?

Obviously in many such cases such opportunities turn into the interesting businesses of the future. But it is not unheard of for them to be nothing more than a **passing fancy** of a boss who is a bit bored with the day job or fears for **their own future** in the company so they want a **Plan B escape** route (but it will more likely be Plan D or E in reality) and then when the job crisis is averted, they quickly forget the partnership leaving the junior members with all the debts and hassle. And being busy people the bosses probably didn't do much if any work at the start either. It can also be dangerous to be left in the firing line of a partnership that is probably breaking some rules or **employment contracts** somewhere along the line, so please beware of working with a boss, it could cost you your job, not improve it.

The Shirt Tails

This kind of partner represents someone who whilst you may **perceive** they have lots of skills and strengths, in practice, it's mostly a blag and they want to partner as they perceive **you** have the stronger skills or work ethic and they hope they can be dragged along by hanging onto your shirt-tails to mutual success. With so many people in business not being what they seem (and you only have to delve skin deep into company accounts via a site like www.companycheck.co.uk to get a shock insight into how even the most successful of businesses are often running on almost thin-air financially), which doesn't speak volumes for most management or their potential as good partners.

The Embarrassed?

I know of more than a view business partnerships that have run into trouble when one party has family or lifestyle issues at **home**, the other member of the partnership (because of a close working relationship) wrongly perceives them to be **friends** and hence offers proactive advice without being asked, or maybe even a financial loan to help them out through tough times.

The result, which I think can only really be explained by the fact the first party is overwhelmed by embarrassment (so lets the event become a big issue that outweighs the importance of the business relationship). Instead, they fall out and don't continue working together. And it can even happen if the supportive gesture was given **reactively** after being asked for help rather than pushed on them as a friend. So maybe the moral here is a sad one, **don't help** people in case it becomes misconstrued? That's just sad.

The Academic

I have been involved with more than a few academics in business and have never had anything but a positive experience but I am aware of people who have seen a different side to things with everything driven by **theory**, rather than pragmatic business sense. Certainly I have experienced the woes of people with just a limited text-book knowledge of a particular aspect of business theory and using that to create the impression they know it all – which would be like me presenting this Bite-Sized Book as everything you could ever need to know about Partnerships as distinct from the far more realistic statement that it's *just one person's knowledge and experience*, make of it what you will by adding in some further research!

A common failure I have heard of from the academic side of things relates to how to manage risk versus budget as in business you rarely have the luxury of getting everything absolutely perfect first time, whatever the text books may say.

But from my experience academic business partners have proved to be totally trustworthy, ethical and have taught me a lot. They also seem to negotiate easily and fairly.

The Over Cautious

With only around 1 in 6 of my potential business partnership relationships being with members of the opposite sex I need here to also draw in some conclusions from my years running an agency too. I have noted that in most cases any activity that involves a large degree of uncertainty or other words, **risk, is likely to be preferred by men**, not women.

I could word this differently and say that in my experience women are more sensible and pragmatic whereas men jump in with both feet, but irrespective of whether this gender stereotype is fair or works for you it is important to consider the risk profile of business partners as **being too cautious will hold you**

back in business, but may conversely save the venture from outright failure.

So in my opinion a mixed approach is best and in my current company I am very happy to have females as fellow shareholders helping me make the best decisions we can together.

> **Editor's note:** It's also important to say that of itself risk in business isn't a bad thing to be avoided at all costs.
>
> **Author's note:** I totally agree. It's managing risk that counts and knowing what you are in for so you can minimise the risk by taking preventive or counter measures. In this way, risk can then be a good thing as it puts competitors off.

The Risk Taker

Obviously a distant black-sheep relative to the above. If you partner with someone who is a huge risk taker it could be the step needed to help you move your business forward much **faster**, but equally these kind of people seem most likely to **drive businesses under** by wrong decisions or actions taken too quickly as they often think nothing of simply starting up again – which doesn't work if you are risk averse. At the very least it makes for a stressful but exciting working environment.

Personally I have probably, on balance, benefited from things like this as we wouldn't have put our business up for sale as early as we did if it had been left to cautious old me, but then again we might have exited better off if we'd waited and grown in the meantime. Who's to say?

One issue to think about with risk is be aware if you are partnering with anyone who has a gambling / casino attitude to life generally as, if they are an avid gambler with their own money, it's important to consider that in a partnership they will potentially have access to do the same with yours. That's another good reason to get your paperwork in order!

The Wealthy

This would surely seem to be the ideal partner as who could help you more in business than someone with cash behind them? And if you partner with someone who is very wealthy and successful it's tempting to assume that whatever else may go wrong in the partnership at least your own finances will be safe? Sadly, this may **not** be the case.

Often very successful people have got that way by hanging onto what they have, tightly – if you've seen the recent film about John Paul Getty (former world's richest man) you will remember how the billionaire had a coin operated phone box installed for guests visiting his stately home! And this happens with partners too – they simply won't stump up their share of debts or volunteer to pay anything first.

I have also seen worse happen and some years ago a newly married friend partnered with an older millionaire. They built a very successful business in a recession, only to have the business go bust as the wealthy one had secretly **embezzled** company funds to support his hobby of collecting old cars, something he could easily have paid for himself from family assets instead.

He also fraudulently switched things like the family home (which was security for the business loan) across into his wife's sole name so when the Bank came knocking to sell it, as they surely would, all the assets had mysteriously gone. The Bank knew what had happened but chose the **easy route** to pay back their debts which was to **ignore multiple frauds** and instead rely on the fact that debts were **jointly and severely** owned by both partners. Hence they repossessed the house off the newly wed, who had done nothing wrong (other than he was the one who introduced the Bank to the business so was easier to find) and he lost everything to pay back debts for both parties even though he had caused none of it. The millionaire wasn't even prosecuted and ended up even wealthier.

On a general note it is worth saying that if **money** is the main thing holding back a business opportunity, then this is available from lots of sources and whilst it is, I suspect, one of the main reasons for picking a partner, it should and could probably be the least important.

Alternative finance routes include:
- Loans from family and friends

- Bank borrowing – preferably unsecured or secured on business physical assets or debts, preferably not your personal assets or tied via a guarantee
- Venture Capitalists, big and small
- Crowd Funding
- Peer to Peer funding – such as Lending Circle
- Invoice Finance (early payment on invoices raised)
- Supplier Finance and long payment terms
- Grants
- Early rebates of VAT or payments for Research and Development expenditure

The Credit Rating

It is not uncommon for partners to be sought out to bolster **something lacking** in the other parties to the business, and this is besides the aforementioned skills, ability or money. This can be things as simple as former bankruptcy, a poor credit rating, an inability to get a Bank account opened or line of credit from an important supplier and plainly these deficits need to be balanced with the **opposite** strength which a partner may provide.

The same is true with **celebrity** partners – I am trying to get one at the moment as this particular asset is vital to help convince the world that an unusual business idea is in fact trusted and real!

This seeming imbalance of effort does not mean you should avoid these kind of partnerships but it is important to try and work out in advance what each party is bringing to the table and what they expect from it in return as once this initial benefit has been donated (without which the business may not even ever get off the ground, and that needs to be remembered) it can be quickly forgotten and eventually resented as it ceases to seem as important as ongoing effort. In summary I think this kind of deal needs to be considered in the same light as having a **sleeping partner** and there is nothing at all wrong with that as long as you realise they will sleep most of the time!

The IPR thief.

I haven't experienced this myself but I am aware of a few people who have partnered with others whose sole intention was to **steal trade secrets** (such as supplier names or prospective client data) or who have even gone as far as to acquiring a business only to then **not pay** for the other party's share when they chose to exit.

And some big brands who I dare not name specialise in acquiring businesses on supposed generous take-over deals only to subsequently **wriggle out** of payments for said business by relying on onerous terms hidden in the **small print** of very cleverly worded contracts. And they do this repeatedly as this is their business model to achieve growth at low cost.

I think the message here is take care if you are dealing with either a serial entrepreneur or a business with a reputation for partnering with and subsequently taking over many businesses. Talk to the former partners and see how they felt about everything a few years down the line, if they can speak freely of course.

Unethical.

It is very difficult, but important, to try and ascertain the ethics of a potential business partner before you jump into any kind of deal. From an obvious perspective this will help ensure you minimise your own personal chances of financial loss but it will also help minimise **stress** within the business, for example caused by the fact some people are comfortable stretching the truth to get a sale, or downright lying, others will go beyond the truth and actually undo a deal by talking about problems that could (but never have) happened. These traits can **apply to anything** from signing contracts, working hours and expenses and it's therefore important to understand that not everyone has the same view or approach on everything.

In one of my businesses, as an example, I had a partner who would delay paying any invoice until the red final demand arrived, so probably 6 months late, whereas my preference is to pay ahead of time or within minutes of being asked – and my philosophy is at least I won't forget (and get an important service cut off by accident) plus if we ever need a favour, said supplier might be more amenable. Ultimately it's just a choice of management style and the other method aids cash-flow / earns interest so it works for some businesses!

Dodgy Deals

Over half a century of deal making and partnerships of various types I estimate that about 10% have gone properly wrong and whilst it feels like a **fraud** of some kind has been committed against me, for example deals being ignored just as if no paperwork existed, in practice lawyers or the other parties might not agree. Either way, I have been very fortunate that none has gone so bad as to necessitate legal action on my part. In addition, the **total** sums lost (only circa **£17,000**, some of which may have even been offset by tax) aren't sufficient to have caused any kind of long-term glitch in our lifestyle or put the family home at risk.

So again, without naming names let's try and put some meat on the bones and categorise what most of these failed partnerships have looked like:

Del Boy.

40% would fit into this category of deal namely they are the kind of people who with hindsight probably never had any intention of honouring any kind of commitment, even on day 1. They probably make commitments like this all the time, maybe it makes them feel good or they simply like getting one over on other people like an unreformed school bully and it makes them feel like a winner every day. Looking back, I can sort of see a consistent personality type here too – **overly friendly and keen initially** yet also full of **self-importance**, but the **friendliness**

outweighs what feels normal for someone of their obvious stature. So watch out for these.

Hard Times.

20% of the bad deals fell into a category whereby I am pretty convinced they were totally honourable people who would **always** honour a deal (and in this case intended to do so at the outset) but with the passage of time they have **hit hard times** or a cash-flow crisis in their business or private lives and hence it is literally (or seems to them) a matter of **survival** to keep every penny to themselves, even if it means reneging on a business deal.

They know it's wrong but feel trapped by circumstance.

So forget trying to collect payments, commissions, investment, whatever have been agreed.

And obviously these are not easy things to talk about afterwards so relationships with said people will often break down too after such an occurrence. It's a shame because in a true partnership, any open discussion about problems would I'm sure be met by an equally open solution with no need to rip partners off from either side of the equation, so for example, a payment plan over a couple of years could be agreed.

It's almost impossibly hard to avoid this kind of scenario – in one real life case I have experienced we no longer correspond, in the other, we do, but I won't be rushing into any new business ventures with the latter as the trust has gone even if they are now back on firm financial footing.

User

Another **20%** of bad deals fit into the category of what I term Users. These are relationships that with hindsight were seemingly set up solely for the intent of **leveraging** your effort or reputation on a specific task with no intent to every carry it forward to a deeper commitment. Companies entering into joint venture partnerships with individuals / smaller businesses seem to fit into this category so look out for anything that feels very task related, gets close to your intellectual property assets or particular skills if they are unique. So that could be things like your contact list, staff training methodology, contract wording, anything really that matters to your specific type of business and that can be accessed to gain profit in the long-term.

The same user philosophy applies to any arrangement that gives instant **credibility** to somebody else, which they can take to the Bank and jettison you later after banking some element of profit, cash or otherwise.

Health.

10% or so feel like real partnerships but have broken down to what I can only assume are unexpected health issues with the other party, sometimes these are physical things like cancer, other times maybe mental or stress related issues leading them to forget what's been agreed. Again these are hard to avoid so it's just the luck of the draw really if you find a partner like this.

Subsidy

The **final 10%** of bad deals are perhaps the weirdest – these are people that enter into a partnership or similar arrangement simply because they perceive there is some kind of **immediate** perk in it for them – and they have no real interest in the business itself. So a made up example of this that might highlight better what I mean would be if I were able to sign up as an employee to British Rail for one hour per month because I then get a travel card allowing me free travel First Class as often as I like – which I then use for my daily commute into London for my day job, which was my primary goal!

In a partnership context I have experienced this happening where people know they want to be travelling regularly somewhere or moving house and here is an opportunity to offset their known future personal costs onto your fledging joint business, plus no doubt a few expenses on the way, and pretend the trip was only for you. In essence it's all about money and I have seen people travel to pick up new cars (claiming thousands on unjustified mileage expenses), subsidise overseas trips (so they can scout out holiday and emigration destinations), buy new laptops (for home) – you name it.

Partnership Upsides

Against a backdrop of 40% of potential partnership deals never actually ended up live, it is a little difficult to draw conclusions **overall** from the 160 or so partner relationships (it's better to focus on the winners which I will do in a moment) but I do realise for anyone considering embarking on partnerships for the first time it may be worth understanding some general conclusions of what you might come up against – if my experience is anything to go by that is.

So with that proviso I have concluded that:

Our **ethics** were only aligned in 40% of cases (and not always the same 60% of ventures that succeeded past the paperwork stage!)

55% of prospective partners proved to be **unreliable** in some way (again, not surprising given that 40% of opportunities ended up going nowhere) and in many cases I was surprised at how many people make **almost no effort** even when they are supposedly embarking upon a new business or opportunity together.

But this leaves an encouraging 45% who proved to be **very reliable** and 40% were IMHO **very ethical** and had ethics similar to my own. The overlap is perhaps unsurprising, over **90%** of those deemed most reliable were also ethical and conversely **68%** of those deemed less than reliable were also less than ethical.

So finding somebody **reliable** would seem to be a first great step towards finding a business partner you can also trust and work with – maybe that's obvious?

This is great as it's relatively easy early on in a relationship to set out and intentionally test whether somebody does what they say they will.

> **Editor's note:** Did you know this already?
>
> **Author's note:** Call me stupid, but no, I hadn't realised it until I crunched the numbers for this book. It's certainly something I will put into practice on future deals before jumping in with both feet and committing to meetings, brainstorming and so on.

There are of course many other upsides from being in partnerships with people, even if they don't end up in profit, hence why I have tried so many of them. I list a few pluses below:

Friendship. Working closely together is a great way to build new friendships and many of mine have endured through thick and thin over **decades**, even if we haven't (yet) enjoyed business success together, as it's not all about business and money.

Work Ethic. It really is a joy to stumble into people with the best kind of attitude and work ethic and I for one think some of this inevitably rubs off onto your own behaviours.

Skills and Knowledge. Ditto – I like learning new things every day and every person I meet (or partner with) is an opportunity to add to my knowledge and experience, which is priceless down the line. And I love working with people who are more intelligent or skilful than me, as I can learn even more new things.

Contacts. In just the same way that when Alexander Graham Bell invented the telephone but could only call his assistant Thomas Watson (to apparently say *Mr Watson, come here please*) as there was nobody else in the phone book, the addition of new contacts creates a multiplier effect as each new subscriber then has multiple more people they could contact. The same is true of partnerships and each new relationship brings with it a wealth of further contacts for your own address book, real or virtual.

Motivational. I mentioned in my introduction that one key reason why I seek out partners is that I find it motivational and hence it spurs me to achieve more for fear of letting them down. So I benefit too.

Chances of Success

In business generally it's regarded as the norm for 80% of businesses to fail within five years, and that's irrespective of how they are set up. it's unsurprising then I suppose for me to have seen a 40% failure rate (failure to launch) over a 50 year period.

Amongst the 60% or so of my own partnership experiences that did proceed past a paperwork only stage, **around one third** ended up in success, so that's around **18% in total** of all opportunities which I regard as a pretty good hit-rate.

What is even more impressive to me is the fact that **each** successful partnership opportunity was worth around **£68,000** to the family coffers, so certainly worth the effort. (This is at 2018 prices)

Chances of Breakeven

As already mentioned, in my experience, the majority of partnership type discussions and agreements will not end in a successful business or indeed any kind of live business. On the plus side of the equation it has to be said that this failed 80% will also have cost almost nothing but a bit of wasted time.

Some of the partnerships (circa 17%) did of course proceed and end in a largely breakeven position (within say a hundred pounds) so that means the overall proportion of partnership opportunities delivering a breakeven position or better adds up to around **65%** so in my experience losing no money is a strong contender as the likely **majority outcome** of partnership discussions, which to me suggests they might take up time but are nothing to fear. You will waste some time and effort but hopefully no money.

Chances of Failure

This of course leaves a percentage as the balance or price of **failure** in partnerships, but not all failures come equal. Maybe I have been lucky or just diligent enough to avoid any major scamsters or fraudsters but amongst the 24 or so deals or partnerships that could be considered to have lost us money, even then **60% fall into the category of small losses**, averaging just

£450 each, and the remaining 40% of what I would term **proper failures** still only lost or more accurately cost us as our share **£1,545 each**, so our total losses over 50 years are still only around **£17,300 over 50 years**. That's a princely **£1 per day!**

> **Editor's note:** But what's the final score on the doors?
>
> **Author's note:** As always you have hit the nail on the head with the key question. It would appear that **for every £1 we have lost** through various failed business initiatives, **we have made up £50 from the successful ones**.

So if our dear readers follow suit, provided they avoid the big risks or scamsters, that's certainly a pattern worth trying to repeat, in **monetary** terms anyway.

> **Editor's note:** What do you mean by that?
>
> **Author's note:** Well I couldn't begin to calculate the time commitment and effort of all these live / failed businesses and partnerships. Much of it is of course done in my spare time but I bet if I added it all together it's only paid me about £1 per hour, and at what cost to the rest of my life?
>
> **Editor's note:** I've done the calculation for you – if you'd invested **every** single spare minute of **every** day into your partnerships etc, and I don't think that's even physically possible, you would still on average have done **better than minimum wage**, so it proves to me

anyway that successful businesses can pay out well.

Outcome Chart

I don't know about you but sometimes with so much math floating about I think it's no bad thing to try and visualise things as a picture, so I have roughly mapped what I saw as the outcomes of all my various partnerships adventures onto the following: each circle represents roughly the size of the number of partners (122 in all across 160 opportunities) at each stage.

As you can see, roughly 60% of opportunities got started and almost a third (18% in the **darkest circle**) became successful, interestingly almost a quarter of these relationships came in from **acquired businesses** with half of that many coming from **staff** I worked with. Other categories of partner are represented at the average levels.

The other point to note I think is the **white circle** whereby roughly 10% went bad or were (to me) fraudulent deals in some way. Noteworthy here is a seeming bias for these relationships to have come about mostly from **networking** or **suppliers** I worked with. As before, other categories of partner are represented at the average statistical levels prevalent roughly equally across all outcomes.

PARTNERSHIP OUTCOMES

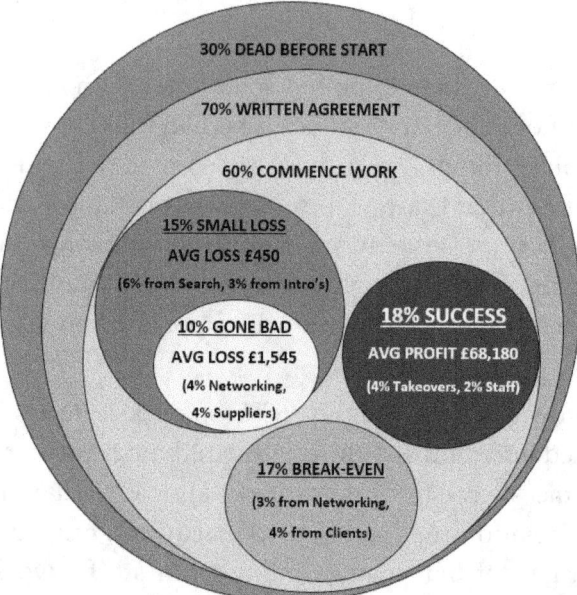

Best Partners to Pick

Assuming success is the goal and that my experience mirrors the norm then the most likely source of relevant and good partners seemed to come from people I knew well in a **work environment.** So these relationships either occurred because they had joined the team as part of a business we acquired (so this is going to be most relevant advice to anyone in a bigger company or part of a Group) and to a lesser degree they were either staff members directly under my employ or other close colleagues. So I **got to see their work closely at first hand.**

Academics, **Bosses** and people I met through **MLM** also seem to be disproportionately represented in this success group, albeit to a lower percentage likelihood of success than the aforementioned groups.

Noticeable for an almost complete **absence** in the success group (or at least less represented than the average) are people being directly **introduced** to me or **Suppliers**.

> **Editor's note:** does that suggest that people keep the best leads for themselves first?!

Author's note: you may have a very valid point –
they only refer on stuff that's less likely to succeed, to me anyway!

Worst Partners to Pick

I won't bother dwelling on those potential partners who seem most destined to create a break-even scenario or even a small loss, neither of which is that life changing financially other than to say that the typical profile seems broadly **similar** being slightly skewed in favour of partners introduced via **Networking**, found via **Search** or as **Clients**, plus a smattering of old **Friends and Neighbours**.

Of more concern are the likely partners that seem inclined to create a greater propensity to **lose money** and in my experience these were much more strongly weighted towards being **Suppliers** or introduced via **Networking** – so I suppose in both cases these are strangers to a degree.

This is not to say success doesn't happen with strangers as everyone is a stranger at first (and indeed MLM contacts will often be unknown to you, but may even then still be well known to somebody close to you) but it does suggest greater caution is required with people who are outside the tent rather than in it with you on a daily basis.

In short, success versus failure seems much more likely if you **know the people well,** but not necessarily as well as family (as that introduces all manner of new biases to succeed and fail), but they are **not selling to you or old friends**!

Hints and Tips

So far we may have unearthed where the potential partners with the best propensity towards your success may lie, and just as importantly where they are not.

We have also discovered that it is probably a good idea to lay a few **traps** requiring effort as if you can catch people out by seeing who gets stuff done and who doesn't it will save hassle and wasted time or money down the line.

So this can either be in the form of getting **comments** on a proposed commercial or legal agreement (more on that in a moment) or maybe something as simple as sending them a few bits to **read** and asking for comments. It takes just minutes to do a quick bit of research on Google, unearth a smart-arse **question** or two and send them off as if you've been really busy and engaged. You do plan actively eventually of course but only when you see the other party is a doer rather than a talker.

So what else is a good idea?

I have always found it's a great initial topic to get people who are prospective business partners to consider four particular aspects as follows:

- Why are we doing this?
- Who are we doing it to and why?

- Who (from the partners) will contribute what exactly?
- What is the exit plan?

Let's looks at these aspects in a little more detail as to why I think they are important:

Why are we doing this?

You have already seen how I have experienced a high reject rate before projects even start (40%) and most of this drop off occurs even before paperwork is agreed. One reason for this is I think it's a good discipline to actively try and work out before hand why you want to be in a partnership in the first place.

So for example is it all about **money**, is it for the **fun** and experience of working together, is it to simply **change the world?** If you can't agree at this early stage or the question is a complete shock to the other party, then I would suggest you are not destined to work together anyway as it isn't a serious enough business or opportunity.

Who are we doing it to and why?

This then narrows the same question down but focusses onto a target **customer** or target **audience**, and beyond that tries to work out what is the partnership's proposed **unique selling point** or proposition.

In other words, **why bother** when the world is so full of other choices? And these questions matter whether your proposed partnership is intended as a profit making business, a charity or a not for profit organisation as, if you don't know who you are trying to satisfy or who is already in that space, how can you hope to succeed?

What do we each contribute?

Again, another ripe area for disagreement and it's a very good idea to iron this aspect out at the outset, particularly if the inputs or work planned are unbalanced in anyway as what starts out as a warm and fuzzy relationship with everyone on the same side can quickly **deteriorate** if one party feels the others are taking advantage and not contributing so much. It's fine if the work or contribution isn't equal, **provided** it is understood and negotiated that way at the outset. It's often very poisonous if not.

In my experience it is better to detail at the outset as close as possible exactly who will contribute what and for how long. That way there are no misunderstandings later to undermine the partnership.

The Exit Plan.

This is generally a surprising aspect to many people as beyond a broad concept of *let's start a business and get rich,* they never give any great thought as to how to do so. This is important to consider as once you have decided on an exit plan this in turn can help reveal ideas about how, when, why, and to whom you might exit, which will help define the partnerships products, services, and prices.

It's also another source of **conflict** so if for example one partner wants to sell out in 48 months, even if only for a modest financial return, but the other wants to create a job for life and create opportunities for their grandchildren, or wait till the business is worth £10 million, these aspirations are hugely out of alignment and this is another aspect that is better cleared up at the outset.

This kind of topic takes some deep thought and maybe even soul searching so it is another great task to set at the outset to help sort the **wheat from the chaff**. Serious partners will do the homework, pretend partners won't.

I have come across so many exit plans in my time ranging from become a millionaire or billionaire in X years, sell out to Microsoft, create a job into retirement, contribute something meaningful back into society, through to change the world – that nothing surprises me.

But it may surprise you if you don't ask the question and have your own answer ready – and if you get these goals in reasonable alignment across partners it really can help create success.

> **Editor's note:** Have you been in partnerships where this wasn't aligned?
>
> **Author's note:** I have. I thought they were aligned at the outset as partners weren't fully transparent, only for a difference to appear over the years. It didn't cause huge issues as I exited part way through (for a profit) but with

hindsight I have since realised how some business decisions we made were indeed influenced by the aforementioned unseen elephant in the room. We would I'm sure have done even better if everything had been discussed and aligned openly up front.

With Hindsight

Now all that analysis is out of the way it's probably a good time to reflect back on my own partnership experiences and consider then how I might do things differently if I was starting all over again.

Firstly, I probably **wouldn't bother** with early attempts at partnership when I was **too young** as other than being good from an experience point of view, as the data seems to have shown, the chance of success with friends, family or neighbours is much lower.

Secondly, as alluded too previously it's certainly a great idea to **test** prospective partners as early in the process as possible to ascertain if they are a doer or just a talker. This can be easily done by exploring the aforementioned questions about: what kind of business is this, why are we doing it, who does what, how do we exit?

By bringing such questions ahead of significant investment or effort on your own part, it should increase the failure rate but reduce wasted budget and wasted time expended in meetings, brainstorming, creating business plans or agreements. This in turn **frees up more time** and resources for the ventures with a chance of going somewhere positive.

Thirdly, given the increased propensity for a venture to go bad or just break-even I would certainly **downgrade** any effort to find prospective partners through **networking** and maybe from Search, Introductions and Suppliers too as in these cases the boot often seems to be on the wrong foot.

Fourth, a greater focus on **Staff, Colleagues, Bosses** and people *discovered* through things like **Business Acquisitions** seems a sensible area to boost finding people interested in something *extracurricular* alongside their day jobs, provided you have enough time and opportunity to **really assess** fully their quality of work, ethics and attitude.

Fifth, contacts formed through **Multi Level Marketing** do appear to have fared better than average as people prepared to make an effort to get ahead so I would probably make an **increased push** in this area, even if I subsequently did **not progress with the MLM opportunity** through which we met but sought to partner on something more traditional instead. Success amongst MLM partners overall was around **two-thirds**.

> **NB.** My Bite-Sized Book **MLM 101** explores the risks, opportunities and pitfalls of MLM as a business choice.

Sixth, Academics are a great source of knowledge, contacts and of course add instant credibility so with hindsight I would have made more effort to **partner with Academics** with the proviso that I would want to ensure they are also well grounded in the ways of **real business**, profit-and-loss and that kind of thing, not just theory, as that luxury alone can prove expensive to fund.

Seventh, I would give partnerships with **Companies** and **Investors** a bit of a **wider berth** and rather than viewing these as a panacea for increased success, I think the opposite is actually true – they have their own **prior agenda** and hence even though it's tempting to think they have aligned goals, this will not always be the case. So before working with such partners I would want **greater clarity** regarding these aspects and things like **exit plans** before starting.

Legal View

When creating my first ever Partnership Agreement I happened to ask the lawyer for his general thoughts and opinions, this being **after** the contractual work was finished, so it was probably an unusual question and he was a little taken aback.

This surprising comment is what he said:

> *This contract captures the spirit of what you are trying to achieve but I would suggest you view it as that, just the spirit.*
>
> *Try and run the business on the basis of a handshake agreement (with people you like and trust) and don't ever rely on any contract to be completely watertight and stand up in court.*
>
> *Any lawyer worth his salt can find something to challenge, especially in a lengthy contract, enabling people to wriggle out of almost anything if they are prepared to pay enough in fees to do so, which they will if it matters enough or is worth enough.*
>
> **So it's better to focus on finding the right partners than the right wording** *and if you ever think you might* **really** *need the paperwork, my suggestion is* **don't proceed** *at all!*

Template Agreement

I have used derivatives of the following document several times. In this instance it is described as a Marketing Venture (to make doubly sure it is not a broader Partnership as I had some doubts about the co-partner's stability) but it could equally be used in a partnership context.

MEMORANDUM of UNDERSTANDING
Re Partnership Name (PN)

A JOINT MARKETING VENTURE BETWEEN

Profitable Partnering of Suites 14-15, Hall Farm, Sywell Aerodrome Business Park, Northants NN6 0BN (Registered Office: As above)

And **The Reader trading as XXXXXXXXX** of XXXXXXXXXXXX (Address)

1 **GENERAL JOINT VENTURE ARRANGEMENT.**

    1.1 WHEREAS **Profitable Partnering** (PP) provides Advice and Statistical Analysis about

Partnership Types and General Business Advice

1.2 AND WHEREAS **The Reader** (TR) provides an Interested and Committed Audience and an Open Mind with regard to learning about these examples of partnership success and failure.

1.3 Profitable Partnering & The Reader collaborate together to promote PN various services and to share the profits from the manufacture and marketing of said services in accordance with the following schedule:

- (a) Upon the commencement of the project, Profitable Partnering are allocated rights to acquire at issue price 2.5% non-voting equity, the remaining 97.5% to remain held by The Reader. Until vested 100% of shares remain held by The Reader.
- (b) Upon successful creation and setting live of a trading website following assistance provided by Profitable Partnering a further allocation of rights over 2.5% equity is awarded to Profitable Partnering.
- (c) Upon successful creation of the business launch a further allocation of rights over 2.5% equity is awarded to Profitable Partnering.

(d) Upon successful sale, merger, floatation of the business or similar or the achievement of net after tax profits in excess of £100,000 pa (or equivalent if value is stored in unusual levels of asset accumulation) this being calculated after allowing for salary payments to The Reader & Family (up to a further £100,000 pa, any excess being factored back into this profit calculation) the allocation of a final 2.5% right to acquire non-voting equity, making 10% maximum in total.

1.4 For the avoidance of doubt, all liabilities and operating costs of the business, build costs for the website, and marketing costs beyond the initial phase are to be paid by PN, any contribution from Profitable Partnering being attributed only when equity rights have been qualified and taken up by profitable Partnering, at which point the Profitable Partnering contribution will be in direct pro-rata contribution to the level of equity rights taken up.

1.5 Any taxes due on the shares taken up by Profitable Partnering resulting by virtue of them being acquired at the issue price, not the prevailing value at the time rights are taken up will be paid by Profitable Partnering.

1.6 In the event that PN continues to trade beyond a two year period and has not been sold, merged, floated or similar, any profits above the afore mentioned £100,000 (after the same calculation for salaries) are to be paid as dividends allocated in a proportion pro-rata to the share allocation rights between Profitable Partnering and The Reader, irrespective of whether rights have been claimed.

1.7 If PN opt not to pay dividends that would otherwise be due under such a calculation, for example, to retain cash in the business for growth, said dividend will remaining owing to Profitable Partnering and be noted in company accounts or similar records if not incorporated as an outstanding loan attracting interest at 5% pa.

1.8 This agreement survives any change in company status or shareholding and for the avoidance of doubt if shareholding does change, mutual dilution occurs with the equity or equivalent held by The Reader pro-rata with that held by Profitable Partnering

1.9 This agreement confers no further or deeper relationship between the parties or over any other business or personal assets or liabilities than those of the PN business and is a marketing arrangement in recognition of professional services rendered by Profitable Partnering to PN – it does not create a broader partnership, the business is wholly owned by The Reader and this agreement simply represents a way of calculating future remuneration for past services provided either at sale or creation of a profitable business in lieu of fee payment now..

2 VOTING.

2.5 Profitable Partnering have no votes in the operation of PN and our services are provided in an advisory capacity only in return for this fee structure linked to future milestones

3 EXIT.

3.5 Profitable Partnering will provide all reasonable assistance to help The Reader sell the business via IPO or similar and will use our best endeavours to recommend strategies that maximise this value and multiples. The Reader on behalf of PN acknowledges that no single strategy will be best or guaranteed to work, there is always a margin of error to be considered.

4 OTHER TERMS.

Unless otherwise agreed, either party is responsible for their own share or charges and disbursements

4.5 The Joint Marketing Venture will commence on signing of this Memorandum and remain in perpetuity with the following exceptions:

4.5.1 The Joint Venture will terminate without notice if either party should be made aware of any gross misconduct relating to the financial operation of the other in any way whatsoever

4.5.2 Profitable Partnering are blacklisted and the website/s banned

    4.5.3   PN or The Reader are the subject of a successful prosecution for patent or similar infringement by the owners of similar products

For the avoidance of doubt such a termination will not avoid either parties or the businesses outstanding financial obligations to the other party

4.6   Should either party decide to sell part or all of their respective businesses to a third party this arrangement should form part of that transfer/sales contract

4.7   Neither party can veto the other parties right to sell their share of the business once a 12 month period has elapsed, and the other party must be given first refusal to purchase at the same price as any external party. Or if disagreement arises, a price agreed by independent arbitrator.

4.8   Shares or equity rights will be passed onto next of kin who have the option to take an equally active part in the business in the event that either party dies or is seriously debilitated

4.9   The jurisdiction of this agreement is the United Kingdom

4.10   If any single clause or section of this agreement should fail a legal challenge it is acknowledged and agreed by both parties that this shall not be detrimental to the enforcement of remaining terms or the general essence of the agreement as adjudicated by independent arbitration

5 COMPENSATION.

5.5 Either party will issue an invoice for their agreed costs or payments, where appropriate, by return

5.6 Deductions for profit calculation purposes include all reasonable direct expenses including cost of product, sales, licensing royalties, hosting charges, credit card & bank charges/services, apportioned audit costs, call handling and phone costs, website development, SEO costs including disbursements plus any further additional costs **agreed jointly** by the parties

6 MONITORING.

6.5 Full reporting on the monthly orders, income and profits will be made available to both parties within ten days of the end of each quarter

6.6 Either party grants full access to the related audited financial data to the other party as required

7 LIABILITY TO THE OTHER PARTY.

The Joint Venture does not in any way imply or constitute a joint or several liability – financial or other – between the parties to any third-party whatsoever nor does it imply or constitute a deeper liability than involvement in this business marketing venture as defined by the restrictions stated

SIGNATURE   SIGNATURE

NAME   NAME

POSITION   POSITION

DATE   DATE

Template Acquisition Document

Whilst this book is primarily about starting Partnerships afresh, as the conclusions suggest finding partners from business **acquisitions** could be an increased source of success, I thought it might be nice to share an example of the kind of simple paperwork I have used to complete 90% of my various business acquisitions and sales.

The exception was a 500 page monster legal agreement supplied by a leading law firm for a mere £25,000. But even with my limited legal skills I spotted 3 or 4 loop-holes in said document that we could exploit latter if needed, which kind of confirms the earlier legal view about the value of contracts.

Since this experience I have preferred to go simple and short – the paperwork that is!

I hope the template is useful to you but as before ,please seek your own legal opinion rather than copying this piecemeal.

BUSINESS TRANSFER AGREMENT

THIS AGREEMENT is made the 11th day of February 2018

BETWEEN **The Reader** (herein called the Seller) of

Partnership Name whose registered office and trading address is XXXXXX (herein called the Transferor) of one part and Profitable Partnering whose trading office is Suites 14-15 Hall Farm, Sywell Aerodrome, Sywell, Northants NN6 0BN (hereinafter called the Transferee) of the other part.

WHEREAS:

a) The Transferor has hitherto carried on business as, inter alia a Advice and Statistical Analysis Writer and General Business Advice supplier hereinafter called the Business; and

b) The Seller has agreed to sell and the Transferee has agreed to purchase the complete issued share capital of Partnership Name whose registered office and trading address is XXXXXXXXX, goodwill (if any) and intellectual property (including but not limited to computer code and associated websites) of the Business upon the terms and for the consideration herein set out.

NOW IT IS HEREBY AGREED as follows:

1) THE Transferor as beneficial owner shall sell and the Transferee shall purchase on a going concern basis, sold "as is" and subjected to limited warrantees as detailed, indemnities or any other liability whatsoever, at and from the close of business on the day of the 11th February 2018 (hereinafter called the Transfer

Date) the Business and all the undertaking, property and assets of the Transferor on the transfer date including (but without prejudice to the generality of the foregoing):

a) The goodwill of the Business (if any) including but not limited to the exclusive right to represent the Transferee as carrying on business in succession to the Transferor, for the avoidance of doubt other than through Companies House records no overt communication about said transfer is intended for 12 months from the Transfer Date and any sales of the products and services of the Transferor company by the Transferee in this interim period will be facilitated as a branded reseller;

b) The intellectual property (including but not limited to computer code and associated websites) of the Business (if any) including but not limited to the exclusive right to represent the Transferee as carrying on business in succession to the Transferor through continuance of its websites, reporting and any other means, all trademarks, registered designs, copyrights and any other rights and interests of whatsoever nature relating to the Business;

c) All plant, equipment, computers, furniture, fixtures and fittings and other chattels of the Transferor owned by the Business and used by it in connection with the Business;

d) All work in progress (if any) relating to the Business;

e) The full benefit (subject to the burden) of all quotations, contracts, engagements and orders subsiding in connection with the Business including (but without prejudice to the generality of the foregoing) the right to receive all income arising thereunder;

f) But to exclude any outstanding Directors Loans, Bank Loans, Invoice Finance, PAYE or NI balances due which will remain with the Transferor on business conducted before the said Transfer Date.

2) THE Transferee shall observe and perform all the obligations of the Transferor in respect of or arising under the quotations, contracts, engagements, orders and other agreements hereby agreed to be transferred and shall indemnify and keep the Transferor indemnified against all actions, proceedings, costs, claims, damages and demands in

respect thereof.

3) THE Transferor provides no undertaking, or representations whatsoever (excepting those detailed) and beyond these the Transferee shall have no recourse to the Transferor.

4) THE consideration for the sale and purchase hereunder shall be £25,000 (fifteen thousand pounds) to be paid on the Transfer Date followed by 12 (twelve) monthly instalments of £1,750 (seven hundred and fifty pounds) on or before the last day of each calendar month when due and paid by bank transfer (the first being due 11th March 2018). It is a further consideration of the sale that on the Transfer Date a number of new shares equivalent to 7% (seven) of the equity value of the Transferee will be assigned to The Reader and Mrs Reader in the ratio 50%/50%

5) In further consideration for the sale and purchase and subject to hitting a turnover (net of bad debt) of £200,000 (twenty five thousand pounds) in the 12 months period (twelve) following the Transfer Date a further 3% (three) equity value will be allocated on the same basis, this benefit being pro-rated

down if less than this target is achieved. Further financial payments will also be made during the period of months 13-24 (thirteen to twenty four) from the Transfer Date at 20% (twenty) of turnover (based on cleared funds received) falling to 15% (fifteen) during the period of months 25-36 (twenty five to thirty six) from the Transfer Date.

6) Furthermore, shares issued in the Transferee will be a new class of share with voting, equity and dividend rights, the latter being agreed annually by the majority shareholder. In addition, further shares may be allocated in recognition of exceptional performance in the continuation of the business post the business transfer date. For the avoidance of doubt the majority shareholder again drives these decisions.

7) Any outstanding monies, however occurring, and due from the Transferor to The Readers at the Transfer Date are waived by them without recourse.

8) THE Transferor will arrange for simultaneous action by The Readers to transfer 100% of the share ownership in the Transferor into the Transferee name and appoint Stuart Haining

as a Director of the Transferor from the Transfer Date. A similar action will be taken with regard to Bank or Finance Company mandates.

9) The Readers simultaneously acknowledge that at the Transfer Date they have compromised their rights under UK Employment Legislation, are effectively resigning from the Transferor business of their own volition and waive any right to be re-employed by the Transferee, they also acknowledge that they are waiving any continuance of employment rights or redundancy terms in lieu of the financial and equity consideration being made. They also acknowledge that at the Transfer Date they have waived any and all reward, salary, compensation, expenses, company shares, other benefits and the like due to them from the Transferee or Transferor except as specified herein.

10) THE Transferee shall accept on good faith the Transferors' declaration and associated undertakings that the business assets for sale, including but not limited to intellectual property, computer code, goodwill and retained clients are indeed theirs to sell. Should a defect in title arise, it is the

responsibility of the sellers The Readers to recompense any damaged party.

11) The completion of the transfer hereunder (hereinafter called "Completion") shall take place on the Transfer Date when the Transferor shall;

   a) Have exchanged the documents and shares outlined herein

   b) Have commenced hand-over of the Transferor company systems to the Transferee company nominated staff member or consultant and agree to provide on-going support to an acceptable level (independent arbitration to be used in the event that a dispute arises as to the extent of this handover and support)

   c) So far as is practicably possible (given that the Transferor business will continue day to day operations by its current directors The Readers) make and give physical delivery and possession of the property and assets agreed to be transferred. In the case of leased or intangible assets, letters of authority and password handover will suffice.

    d) Commence weekly management reporting of performance and high level metrics to the Transferee

12) THE Transferor shall upon completion or following completion at the shared expense of the Transferee execute or do so procure to be done all such assurances and things as are reasonably required by the Transferee for vesting in it the property as assets hereby agreed to be sold to the Transferee.

13) THE Transferor shall notify the Transferee of any standing orders, direct debits, credit card mandates or other forms of regular payment in order that revised payment instructions can be submitted to facilitate the smooth running of the Business and services going forward. Should any advance payments be required to be made by the Transferor prior to the Transfer Date in relation to services delivered after said Transfer Date, provided the Transferee has been made aware of such a payment and agrees it is necessary to facilitate the seamless transfer and continuation of the Business, then pro-rata payment will be made to reimburse the Transferor.

14) INSOFAR as any consent or sanction of any third party is required to the transfer of any

property, assets, intellectual property and computer code, rights, obligations, benefits or burdens of the Transferor hereunder and such consent shall not have been received to the satisfaction of the Transferee at completion:

a) Nothing in this agreement shall operate as such a transfer or assignment as would give rise to any termination or forfeiture of any benefit, right or interest to any person in any of the said property or assets;

b) In the event of any such consent or sanction being refused or not being received to the satisfaction of the Transferee in respect of subsisting quotations, contracts, engagements, orders or other agreements the Transferor shall execute and perform the same as required by the Transferee and shall continue to do so as an agent for and on behalf of the Transferee until such consent or sanction is received or full performance shall have been given in respect thereof and so that any profits or losses arising there-from shall be for the benefit or burden (as the case maybe) of the Transferee.

15) IF by reason of the absence of any consent or sanction required for any other reason whatsoever the title to or benefit of any of the property or assets of the Transferor the subject of this agreement is not transferred to the Transferee at completion, the Transferor shall until title thereto has been finally and effectively vested in the Transferee hold the same upon trust for the benefit of the Transferee absolutely. The Transferor will make good any financial losses proved to have been suffered by the Transferee as a direct result of said shortcoming from the Transfer Date until the date of resolution – said matter being referred to independent arbitration as necessary

16) THE parties hereto acknowledge that this agreement constitutes a relevant transfer for the purposes of the Transfer of Undertakings (Protection of Employment) Regulations and accordingly shall not operate so as to terminate the contract of employment of any person, including Directors, employed by Transferor nor have any such employment changes been made within the preceding 3 month (three) period prior to the Transfer Date. Any such contract or contracts which would otherwise have been terminated by the

Transfer shall have the effect as if they were originally made between the person so employed and the Transferee. Such amount as represents the outstanding holiday entitlement (if any) of such an employee at the Transfer Date shall constitute a liberty for the purpose of clause 2 above and as such shall have been deemed waived by the recipient.

17) EACH party shall bear their own costs and expenses in respect of this agreement and carrying the same into effect.

18) This agreement shall be governed by English law and all disputes shall be resolved by English Courts. In the event that any single element of this agreement is deemed unenforceable, this shall not be to the detriment of other elements of the agreement, as appropriate being replaced by suitably reworded elements designed to facilitate essentially the same agreement.

19) If either party to this agreement has been deemed to have acted fraudulently or miss-represented either themselves or the assets and businesses within the undertaking this

agreement will be deemed null and void with the offending party required to make appropriate financial recompense to the other party to reset the status as if said actions had not occurred. In all cases the total limit of any compensation payable by the Seller shall be equivalent to the value of the consideration detailed in paragraph 3, including the return of title to any shares in the Transferees business issued to the Seller as part of the sale.

20) Only limited warranties apply to this agreement and they are as follows:

a) The intellectual property of the Business is owned wholly by The Readers

b) The previous owners of the Business have no remaining influence over the transfer of assets or this agreement.

c) A "corporation tax credit" will be carried forward on completion, all other taxes will be paid to date.

d) Sufficient funds to enable working capital for the next 3 months will remain in the business accounts on transfer

e) The asset list is shown at **Appendix A** to this agreement.

f) The reseller/partner relationships live at the Transfer Date are shown at **Appendix B** to this agreement.

g) Debts outstanding more than 30 days, reasons, and expected payment dates or otherwise at 11/02/2018 are shown at **Appendix C** to this agreement.

h) Risks have been identified and notified to the Transferee as shown in answer to question 19 of **Appendix D** to this document. **Appendix D** also contains questions and answers covered during due diligence.

21) This agreement represents the whole agreement between the Transferor and Transferee and respective signatories, there is no broader relationship impacting other assets of the individuals than outlined in this agreement, save from the fact that the Transferee business also owns a number of other ventures in whole or in part and accordingly in so far as The Readers will be allocated shares in said company, they will therefore also own a minority stake in said ventures, which may or may not infer voting and dividend rights on a case by case basis.

Attached: Appendix A – Asset List and Book Values

Appendix B – Contact List

Appendix C – Debts Outstanding and due

Appendix D – Risks and Due Diligence Q & A (see below)

1) Business owned by whom? Please supply share certificates upon completion.

2) Relevant business addresses? Include Registered details, where Business Rates & Insurance are recorded against.

3) Employee details and contract terms. Have compromise agreements / TUPE undertakings being agreed / signed?

4) Any pending HR issues?

5) Payment agreements re Business Acquisition.

6) Any contractual restrictions in place or agreed.

7) Assets included in sale. Who owns them? Any leases?

8) Any third party actions against the business?

9) Any copyrights, patents, registered rights owned?

10) Statutory Returns and Taxes up to date?

11) Are Management Accounts fair and accurate representations of the business looking forward?

12) Any substantive debts or longer term contractual agreements to buy or supply services amounting to more than £1k, if so, please provide details and expiry dates.

13) Are there any major bad debts owed to the company, by the company beyond a 60 day period.

14) Details of any third party agreements, joint ventures, supply contracts (for example the outsourced contractor) and resellers.

15) Technology hosting, website, email and software licence details and password lists

16) Any commissions arrangements to or from third parties, terms and renewal dates.

17) Any loans due?

18) List of client, partner, reseller, supplier and staff gains and losses over the last 12 months – with reasons and copy of contracts in place for all.

19) Provide simplified process flow diagram explaining how the business operates, eg, processes, relationships, hardware, software interactions so we have a simple path to enable disaster recovery planning.

20) Copies of all Bank and Finance statements.

21) Copies of business acquisition contracts (if you acquired the business rather than started anew)

22) Any other disclosures or warrantees you feel it would be appropriate to get out of the way now!

IN WITNESS whereof

Witness Signature   Name   Title

Address   Date

EXECUTED as a deed by
Stuart Haining, Profitable Partnering

Signature   Date

EXECUTED as a deed by
The Reader

Signature   Date

EXECUTED as a deed by Mrs Reader

Signature   Date

Bite-Sized Business Books are designed to provide practical support and insights for professionals who are tackling an unfamiliar task either for the first time or after a gap, as well as those who want to find new ways of doing what they are familiar with. They are deliberately short, easy to read books guiding the reader through the various stages behind each business process or activity, with a clear focus on outcomes. They are firmly based on personal experience and success.

The most successful people all share an ability to focus on what really matters, keeping things simple and understandable. MBAs, metrics and methodologies have their place, but when we are faced with a new challenge most of us need quick guidance on what matters most, from people who have been there before and who can show us where to start. As Stephen Covey famously said, "The main thing is to keep the main thing, the main thing." But what exactly is the main thing?

Bite-Sized books were conceived to help answer precisely that question crisply and fast and, of course, be engaging to read, written by people who are experienced and successful in their field.

The brief? Distil the *main things* into a book that can be read by an intelligent non-expert comfortably in around 60 minutes. Make sure the book enables the reader with specific tools, ideas and plenty of examples drawn from real life and business. Be a virtual mentor.

Bite-Sized Books don't cover every eventuality, but they are written from the heart by successful people who are happy to share their experience with you and give you the benefit of their success.

We have avoided jargon – or explained it – and made few assumptions about the reader, except that they are in business, are literate and numerate, and that they can adapt and use what we suggest to suit their own, individual purposes. Whether you are working for a multi-national corporation or a start-up or something in between, the principles we introduce will hold good.

They can be read straight through at one easy sitting and then used as a support while you are working on what you need to do.

Bite-Sized Books Catalogue

Business Books

Ian Benn
> Write to Win
>> How to Produce Winning Proposals and RFP Responses

Matthew T Brown
> Understand Your Organisation
>> An Introduction to Enterprise Architecture Modelling

David Cotton
> Rethinking Leadership
>> Collaborative Leadership for Millennials and Beyond

Richard Cribb
> IT Outsourcing: 11 Short Steps to Success - An Insider's View

Phil Davies
> How to Survive and Thrive as a Project Manager
>> The Guide for Successful Project Managers

Paul Davies
> Developing a Business Case
>> Making a Persuasive Argument out of Your Numbers

Paul Davies
> Developing a Business Plan
>> Making a Persuasive Plan for Your Business

Paul Davies
> Contract Management for Non-Specialists

Paul Davies
> Developing Personal Effectiveness in Business

Paul Davies
> A More Effective Sales Team
>> Sales Management Focused on Sales People

Tim Emmett
> Bid for Success
>> Building the Right Strategy and Team

Nigel Greenwood
> Why You Should Welcome Customer Complaints
>> And What to Do About Them

Nigel Greenwood
> Six Things that All Customer Want
>> A Practical Guide to Delivering Simply Brilliant Customer Service

Stuart Haining
> The Practical Digital Marketeer – Volume 1
>> Digital Marketing – Is It Worth It and Your First Steps

Stuart Haining
> The Practical Digital Marketeer – Volume 2
>> Planning for Success

Stuart Haining
> The Practical Digital Marketeer – Volume 3
>> Your Website

Stuart Haining
> The Practical Digital Marketeer – Volume 4
>> Be Sociable – Even If You Hate It

Stuart Haining
> The Practical Digital Marketeer – Volume 5
>> Your On-going Digital Marketing

Stuart Haining
> Profitable Partnerships
>> Practical Solutions to Help Pick the Right Business Partner

Christopher Hosford
> Great Business Meetings! Greater Business Results
>> Transforming Boring Time-Wasters into Dynamic Productivity Engines

Ian Hucker
> Risk Management in IT Outsourcing
>> 9 Short Steps to Success

Alan Lakey
- Idiocy in Commercial Life
  - Practical Ways to Navigate through Nonsense

Marcus Lopes and Carlos Ponce
- Retail Wars
  - May the Mobile be with You

Maiqi Ma
- Win with China
  - Acclimatisation for Mutual Success Doing Business with China

Elena Mihajloska
- Bridging the Virtual Gap
  - Building Unity and Trust in Remote Teams

Rob Morley
- Agile in Business
  - A Guide for Company Leadership

Gillian Perry
- Managing the People Side of Change
  - Ten Short Steps to Success in IT Outsourcing

Saibal Sen
- Next Generation Service Management
  - An Analytics Driven Approach

Don Sharp
- Nothing Happens Until You Sell Something
  - A Personal View of Selling Techniques

Lifestyle Books

Anna Corthout
>Alive Again
>>My Journey to Recovery

Phil Davies
>Don't Worry Be Happy
>>A Personal Journey

Phil Davies
>Feel the Fear and Pack Anyway
>>Around the World in 284 Days

Stuart Haining
>My Other Car is an Aston
>>A Practical Guide to Ownership and Other Excuses to Quit Work and Start a Business

Stuart Haining
>After the Supercar
>>You've Got the Dream Car – but is it Easy to Part With?

Bill Heine
>Cancer – Living Behind Enemy Lines Without a Map

Regina Kerschbaumer
>Yoga Coffee and a Glass of Wine
>>A Yoga Journey

Gillian Perry
>Capturing the Celestial Lights
>>A Practical Guide to Imagining the Northern Lights

Arthur Worrell
> A Grandfather's Story
>> Arthur Worrell's War

Public Affairs Books

Eben Black
> Lies Lunch and Lobbying
>> PR, Public Affairs and Political Engagement – A Guide

John Mair and Richard Keeble (Editors)
> Investigative Journalism Today:
>> Speaking Truth to Power

John Mair, Richard Keeble and Farrukh Dhondy (Editors)
> V.S Naipaul:
>> The legacy

John Mair and Neil Fowler (Editors)
> Do They Mean Us – Brexit Book 1
>> The Foreign Correspondents' View of the British Brexit

John Mair, Neil Fowler and Alex De Ruyter (editors)
> The Case for Brexit

Christian Wolmar
> Wolmar for London
>> Creating a Grassroots Campaign in a Digital Age

Fiction

Paul Davies
> The Ways We Live Now
>> Civil Service Corruption, Wilful Blindness, Commercial Fraud, and Personal Greed – a Novel of Our Times

Paul Davies
> Coming To
>> A Novel of Self-Realisation

Children's Books

Chris Reeve – illustrations by Mike Tingle
> The Dictionary Boy
>> A Salutary Tale

Fredrik Payedar
> The Spirit of Chaos
>> It Begins

www.ingramcontent.com/pod-product-compliance
Lightning Source LLC
Chambersburg PA
CBHW071207220526
45468CB00002B/530